W9-DDJ-443

JOBS KIDS WANT

WHAT'S IT REALLY LIKE TO BE A FIREFIGHTER?

CHRISTINE HONDERS

PowerKiDS press.
New York

Published in 2020 by The Rosen Publishing Group, Inc.
29 East 21st Street, New York, NY 10010

First Edition

Editor: Greg Roza
Book Design: Michael Flynn

Photo Credits: Cover, p. 1 Tyler Stableford/Stone/Getty Images; pp. 4, 6, 8, 10, 12, 14, 16, 18, 20, 22 (background) Apostrophe/Shutterstock.com; p. 5 Isaiah Shook/Shutterstock.com; p. 7 (main) sandyman/Shutterstock.com; p. 7 (inset) 7th Son Studio/Shutterstock.com; p. 9 https://commons.wikimedia.org/wiki/File:Raphael_-_Fire_in_the_Borgo.jpg; p. 11 Justin Sullivan/Getty Images; p. 13 Bruno Ismael Silva Alves/Shutterstock.com; p. 15 JRP Studio/Shutterstock.com; p. 17 potowizard/Shutterstock.com; p. 19 Rena Schild/Shutterstock.com; p. 21 Anton Havelaar/Shutterstock.com; p. 22 Jamroen Jaiman/Shutterstock.com.

Cataloging-in-Publication Data

Names: Honders, Christine.
Title: What's it really like to be a firefighter? / Christine Honders.
Description: New York : PowerKids Press, 2020. | Series: Jobs kids want | Includes glossary and index.
Identifiers: ISBN 9781538349885 (pbk.) | ISBN 9781538349908 (library bound) | ISBN 9781538349892 (6 pack)
Subjects: LCSH: Fire extinction–Vocational guidance–Juvenile literature. | Fire fighters–Juvenile literature.
Classification: LCC TH9119.H66 2019 | DDC 363.37023–dc23

Manufactured in the United States of America

CPSIA Compliance Information: Batch #CSPK19. For Further Information contact Rosen Publishing, New York, New York at 1-800-237-9932.

CONTENTS

The Dangers of Fire

Fire is amazing. It gives us heat and light. But fire can be dangerous too. It can ruin homes and forests. It can also kill people. When fire becomes a danger, we call firefighters. It's a firefighter's job to put out fires.

How Does a Fire Start?

Fire needs three things to burn—**fuel**, heat, and **oxygen**. Firefighters put fires out by taking one of these things away. Firefighters take heat away from fire by spraying water on it. They remove oxygen from a fire with fire **extinguishers**.

fire extinguishers

The First Firefighters

There were firefighters in Rome over two thousand years ago! If there was a fire, they lined up by the nearest lake or river. They passed buckets of water to each other. The last firefighter in line dumped the water on the fire.

LEO·PP·IIII

Racing to the Rescue

When the fire alarm goes off, firefighters race to the rescue! They put out the fire and keep it from spreading. They help people who are trapped. They fight wildfires in forests. Firefighters also help in other emergencies, such as car accidents.

FOREST SERVICE

Firefighting Gear

Firefighters use lots of tools. They attach hoses to fire **hydrants** and use water pumps to power the hoses. Pumper trucks carry water pumps and long hoses. Ladder trucks help rescue people in tall buildings. Helicopters drop water on forest fires.

Safety First!

Firefighters wear special helmets, jackets, gloves, and boots to keep themselves safe from heat and flames. They also carry masks with air tanks to help them breathe. Firefighters wear special **devices**. They give out a sound, letting other firefighters know where they are if they need help.

Putting Their Lives in Danger

Firefighters put their lives in danger all the time. They run into burning buildings to rescue people. Some things burned in fires can make firefighters sick. Smoke can cause breathing problems for firefighters. Sometimes these problems last the rest of their lives.

Becoming a Firefighter

To become a firefighter, you need to graduate from high school. Then you need to pass three tests to show you can do the job. Some people go to a firefighting school. Some get their training at the fire station with experienced firefighters.

58

A Day at the Station

Most calls aren't about fires. They're from people who are sick or **injured**. Some firefighters have medical training for emergencies. Firefighters spend lots of time teaching people about fire safety. They show us what to do in case of a fire.

ENGINE COMPANY 4
LADDER COMPANY 15
F.D.N.Y.
www.nyc.gov/fdny
4

Neighborhood Heroes

Firefighters do dangerous work together, so they have to look out for each other. They work hard to keep each other safe. They become like a family. Firefighters risk their lives to save others. They're heroes in our neighborhood!

GLOSSARY

device: A tool that does a certain thing.

extinguisher: A tool that puts out fire by spraying it and cutting off its oxygen.

fuel: Something used to make heat or power (like gasoline or wood).

hydrant: A pipe in the ground with a spout that can be attached to a hose to spray water.

injured: To be hurt or in pain.

oxygen: A colorless, tasteless gas in the air that we need to breathe.

INDEX

WEBSITES

Due to the changing nature of Internet links, PowerKids Press has developed an online list of websites related to the subject of this book. This site is updated regularly. Please use this link to access the list: www.powerkidslinks.com/JKW/firefighter